Desserts

ACADEMIA
BARILLA

The Taunton Press

ACADEMIA BARILLA
AMBASSADOR OF ITALIAN GASTRONOMY
THROUGHOUT THE WORLD

Academia Barilla is a global movement toward the protection, development and promotion of authentic regional Italian culture and cuisine.
With the concept of Food as Culture at our core, Academia Barilla offers a 360° view of Italy. Our comprehensive approach includes:

- a state-of-the-art culinary center in Parma, Italy;
- gourmet travel programs and hands-on cooking classes;
- the world's largest Italian gastronomic library and historic menu collection;
- a portfolio of premium artisan food products;
- global culinary certification programs;
- custom corporate services and training;
- team building activities;
- and a vast assortment of Italian cookbooks.

Thank you and we look forward to welcoming you in Italy soon!

CONTENTS

EDITED BY
ACADEMIA BARILLA

PHOTOGRAPHS
ALBERTO ROSSI

RECIPES BY
CHEF MARIO GRAZIA
CHEF LUCA ZANGA

TEXT BY
MARIAGRAZIA VILLA

ACADEMIA BARILLA EDITORIAL COORDINATION
CHATO MORANDI
ILARIA ROSSI
REBECCA PICKRELL

GRAPHIC DESIGN
PAOLA PIACCO

THE DESSERT NEEDS TO BE SPECTACULAR,
BECAUSE IT IS SERVED WHEN THE
GOURMAND IS NO LONGER HUNGRY.

ALEXANDRE BALTHAZAR LAURENT
GRIMOD DE LA REYNIÈRE,
ALMANACH DES GOURMANDS, 1803-1812

DESSERTS

What would Italian cuisine be without its sweets? Soft, fragrant ricotta cheese tucked into a crispy golden crust. Puff pastry in a cloud of powdery sugar. Pastry with aromatic surprises within. Apples, peaches and strawberries bathed in sweet nectar. Some of the Italian tradition's most delightful creations are its desserts.

Each region of the *Bel Paese* (the "beautiful country," as Italians call their home) has a wealth of typical sweets. They range from simple dishes originating in the kitchens of humble folk to the most elaborate and virtuosic, created in the great Renaissance courts. There are small pastries and spoon desserts; cakes, doughnuts and tarts; ice creams and sorbets; and fruit-based preparations.

The dessert, a term deriving from the old French verb *desservir*, meaning to clear the table, was introduced during the Middle Ages, indicating it closed the meal with sweetness. Initially it consisted of candies or little sweets served with hot spiced wine and aged cheese. Later it included fresh fruit sprinkled with sugar, honey or syrups, and sweets made from cooked fruit.

For this volume, Academia Barilla, an international center dedicated to the preservation and promotion of Italian cuisine, has selected 40 "made in Italy" dessert recipes that are simple to prepare at home.

Nearly all the desserts in this volume are regional flagships that have now become national delicacies: like cannoli, masterpieces of the Sicilian art of pastry; the original *pastiera* (Easter pie), one of the good-luck symbols of Naples; the rustic *sbrisolona* (almond crumb cake), the undisputed pride of Mantua; and the intense Piedmontese bonet, a pudding of amaretti cookies.

Some of these traditional sweets are presented with

slight regional differences. Consider the *castagnaccio*, for example, a cake made from chestnut flour: with minor variations, this recipe is made in Tuscany, Liguria, Piedmont, Emilia, and Lombardy. *Chiacchiere* (angel wings), strips of sweetened dough, fried or cooked in the oven, then sprinkled with sugar, are traditionally prepared during Carnevale, in various versions, all over Italy, where they take on different names as well: *frappe, crostoli, cenci*, and more.

We have also included a relatively new dessert, the tiramisù, beloved throughout Italy and around the world. Created in the late 1960s in a Treviso restaurant, its preparation changes regionally: with cookies or sponge cake instead of ladyfingers; with yogurt or ricotta instead of mascarpone; with barley coffee or fruit juices instead of coffee; with amaretti or coconut instead of cocoa powder.

There are other recipes that are typically Italian, not because of their history but because of the special character of their creation: the deep respect for the quality of their ingredients; the wise balance between tradition and innovation; and the inspiration in marrying ingredients that truly speak to one another. The white chocolate and raspberry tart, and the moscato jelly with berries, for example, are marvels for the eyes as well as for the palate. And the ricotta mousse with almond milk is a hymn to the pastry of Sicily—from that island, after the Arab domination, sprung the "dessert colonization" not only of the entire Italian peninsula but of all of Europe.

LADY'S KISSES

Preparation time: 40 minutes   Resting time: 30 minutes
Cooking time: 15 minutes   Difficulty: medium

4 SERVINGS

1 cup (125 g) **all-purpose flour**
5/8 cup (125 g) **sugar**
3/4 cup (100 g) **roasted hazelnuts**
1/4 cup (25 g) **blanched almonds**
1/2 cup (125 g) **unsalted butter**, *softened*
3/8 cup (30 g) **unsweetened cocoa powder**
3 1/2 oz. (100 g) **dark chocolate**

In a blender, using the pulse feature, finely grind the hazelnuts and almonds with the sugar. In a bowl, mix the resulting powder with the butter. In another bowl, sift the flour and cocoa powder together, then incorporate into the butter mixture, stirring it as little as possible. Wrap the mixture in plastic wrap and refrigerate for at least 30 minutes.

Heat the oven to 325°F (160°C). On a clean, lightly floured work surface, roll out the chilled mixture to a thickness of about 3/8 inch (1 cm). Cut out disks with pastry rings 5/8 to 3/4 inch (1 1/2 to 2 cm) in diameter and shape into balls. Arrange the balls on a lightly buttered, floured baking sheet (or one lined with parchment paper) and bake in the oven for about 15 minutes. Let cool completely, then transfer from the pan and invert them (rounded side down). Meanwhile, melt the chocolate in a heatproof bowl set over a pan of simmering water, or in the microwave. Let it cool until it begins to crystallize. Pour a little on each of half the batch of cookies. Place flatter side of another cookie on top of each and allow the lady's kisses *(baci di dama)* to set.

CREAM PUFFS

Preparation time: 25 minutes   Cooking time: 20 minutes   Difficulty: medium

4 SERVINGS

FOR THE PASTRY
3/8 cup (100 ml) **water**
3 1/2 tbsp. (50 g) **unsalted butter**, *cut
into small pieces, plus more for pan*
1/2 cup (60 g) **all-purpose flour**
2 large **eggs**
Salt

FOR THE CREAM FILLING
2 cups (500 ml) **milk**
3/4 cup (150 g) **sugar**
4 large **egg yolks**
1/8 cup (20 g) **all-purpose flour**
2 1/2 tbsp. (20 g) **cornstarch**
1 **vanilla bean**, *split lengthwise*

In a saucepan, bring the water to a boil with the butter and a pinch of salt. Sift the flour; add it all at once to the boiling water and whisk. When the mixture begins to thicken, stir with a wooden spoon and continue cooking over medium heat for 2 to 3 minutes. Remove from heat, let cool slightly, then beat in the eggs one at a time, incorporating each before adding the next.

Heat the oven to 375°F (190°C).

Using a pastry bag fitted with a smooth tip 1/4 inch (6 mm) in diameter, pipe pastry puffs onto a buttered baking sheet and bake for about 20 minutes. Meanwhile, prepare the filling. Bring the milk to a boil in a saucepan with half the vanilla bean (reserve remaining half bean for another use). Whisk egg yolks with sugar in a bowl. In another bowl, sift the cornstarch and flour together; whisk into egg yolk mixture. Pour a quarter of the boiling milk into the egg yolk mixture and stir until smooth. Add this mixture to remaining milk over medium heat, whisking constantly and returning it to a boil, until thick. Pour the cooked cream filling into a bowl and cool it quickly. Cut off the top of each pastry puff and use a pastry bag to fill with cream.

CHOCOLATE CHIP COOKIES

Preparation time: 20 minutes   Cooking time: 15 minutes   Difficulty: easy

4 SERVINGS

1 1/2 cups (200 g) **all-purpose flour**
1 cup (180 g) **chocolate chips**
1/2 cup (100 g) **sugar**
3/8 cup (90 g) **unsalted butter**, softened
1 large **egg**
1 tsp. (5 g) **baking powder**
1/2 tsp. (3 ml) **vanilla extract**
Salt

Heat the oven to 360°F (180°C).
In a bowl, cream the butter and sugar. Add a pinch of salt, the egg, and the vanilla extract.
Sift the flour with baking powder and add to the butter mixture. Knead mixture with your hands until the dough is smooth. Stir in the chocolate chips.
On a floured surface, form the dough into a length about 1 inch (2 1/2 cm) in diameter.
Cut into pieces and form into balls with your hands.
Line a baking sheet with parchment paper and arrange the balls, spaced at least 1 inch (2.5 cm) apart. Flatten each ball slightly with the palm of your hand.
Bake in the oven for about 15 minutes or until cookies are golden brown.

CHOCOLATE BISCUITS

Preparation time: 20 minutes   *Cooking time: 10-12 minutes*   *Difficulty: easy*

4 SERVINGS

1 cup (125 g) **confectioners' sugar**
1/4 cup (25 g) **unsweetened cocoa powder**
1 large **egg white**
1/2 cup (75 g) **chopped toasted hazelnuts**
2 tbsp. (15 g) **potato starch** *(or cornstarch)*
1 tsp. (5 g) **baking powder**
1/2 tsp. (3 ml) **vanilla extract**

Heat the oven to 340°F (170°C).
Sift together the confectioners' sugar, cocoa, starch and baking powder in a bowl.
Stir in the egg white and vanilla extract until smooth. Add the hazelnuts and stir.
On a lightly floured work surface, form the mixture into a log about 1 1/4 inches
(3 cm) in diameter. Cut into slices 3/8 inch (1 cm) thick.
Butter and flour a baking sheet, or line with parchment paper. Arrange the
biscuits on baking sheet and bake for 10 to 12 minutes.
Let biscuits cool completely before removing from the pan.

BONET
(PIEDMONTESE PUDDING)

Preparation time: 20 minutes   Cooking time: 45 minutes
Cooling time: 2 hours   Difficulty: easy

4 TO 6 SERVINGS

FOR THE PUDDING
1 1/2 cups (375 ml) **milk**
3 large **eggs**
1/2 cup (115 g) **sugar**
1/8 cup (40 ml) **water**
1/4 cup (25 g) **unsweetened cocoa
powder**

1 tsp. (5 ml) **rum**
3 oz. (75 g) **amaretti cookies**

FOR THE CARAMEL
1/2 cup (100 g) **sugar**
2 tbsp. (25 ml) **water**

Heat the oven to 325°F (160°C).
In a pan over medium heat, gently cook the sugar with the water until it turns a deep blonde color, then pour it into a dessert mold or individual molds and let cool.
In another saucepan, boil the milk.
Meanwhile, place the amaretti cookies between 2 sheets of waxed paper and crush into crumbs with a rolling pin.
Whisk the eggs and sugar together in a bowl, then add the cocoa, amaretti crumbs, and rum.
Add the boiling milk, stir, and pour into the caramelized molds.
Place molds in a deep baking pan and add enough hot water to the pan to reach halfway up molds. Bake in the oven for about 45 minutes.
Let the puddings cool in the refrigerator for least 2 hours before you unmold them.

SICILIAN CANNOLI

Preparation time: 30 minutes Resting time: 1-1 1/2 hours
Cooking time: 2 minutes   Difficulty: medium

4 SERVINGS

FOR THE PASTRY
3/4 cup plus 1 tbsp. (100 g) **all-purpose**
flour *or Italian "00" type flour*
2 tbsp. (10 g) **unsweetened cocoa powder**
3 1/2 tsp. (15 g) **sugar**
1 large **egg**
1 tbsp. (15 ml) **Marsala wine** *or rum*
2 tsp. (10 g) **unsalted butter**, *softened*
Salt

FOR THE FILLING
8 3/4 oz. (250 g) **fresh ricotta**,
preferably made from sheep's milk
1/2 cup (100 g) **sugar**
1 oz. (25 g) **candied fruit**, *roughly chopped*
1 oz. (25 g) **chocolate chips**, *or*
semisweet chocolate roughly chopped
1 oz. (25 g) **pistachios**, *roughly chopped*
Olive oil *for frying, as needed*
Confectioners' sugar

To prepare the pastry, combine the flour, cocoa, butter, egg, sugar, and a pinch of salt in a bowl. Turn the mixture out onto a clean work surface, add the marsala and knead until dough is smooth. Let it rest for 30 minutes.

In the meantime, prepare the filling. Run the ricotta through a sieve and combine it with the fruit, chocolate, and pistachios. Wrap in plastic wrap and refrigerate from 30 minutes to 1 hour. Roll out the dough to 1/8 inch (2 mm) thick and cut it into 4-inch (10-cm) squares. Wrap the squares diagonally around a special cannoli form (or stainless-steel dowels cut in 4-inch lengths). Heat oil in a pan until shimmering. Place cannoli form with dough into hot oil and fry until golden, 1 to 2 minutes. Remove from the oil, drain on paper towels, and let cool.

Once shells have cooled, remove them from the cannoli form. Using a pastry bag, fill the cannoli with the ricotta filling, then dust with powdered sugar. Serve immediately (the moist filling soon makes the dough lose its crispness).

ALMOND BISCOTTI

Preparation time: 20 minutes   Cooking time: 20 minutes   Difficulty: medium

INGREDIENTS FOR APPROXIMATELY 1 LB. (450 G) COOKIES

2 cups (250 g) **flour**
7/8 cup (175 g) **sugar**
4 1/2 oz. (125 g) **blanched almonds**
1/2 tsp. (2 g) **baking powder**
2 (95 g) large **eggs** *plus 2 (30 g) large* **egg yolks**
Salt
1 tsp. (5 ml) **vanilla extract** *(or to taste)*

Heat oven to 360°F (180°C). Line a baking pan with parchment paper.
Sift together the flour, baking powder, and a pinch of salt in a large bowl. In a medium bowl, mix sugar, eggs and egg yolk. Add egg mixture to flour mixture and stir until dough is well blended and smooth.
Divide dough in half. On a clean, floured work surface, form dough into logs about 12 inches (30 1/2 cm) long by 2 1/2 (6 cm) inches wide. Place logs on parchment-lined baking pan.
Bake in the oven for about 20 minutes or until golden brown.
Remove the logs from the oven and cut them with a serrated knife into 1/2-inch-wide diagonal slices when still hot. Place the slices, cut side down, on same baking sheet and return to the oven for 10 minutes more, or until golden brown on both sides.

CASSATA
(SICILIAN CHEESECAKE)

Preparation time: 1 hour   Resting time: 3 hours   Difficulty: high

4 SERVINGS

FOR THE CAKE AND RICOTTA CREAM
8 3/4 oz. (250 g) **sheep's-milk ricotta**
1/2 cup (90 g) **sugar**
1 oz. (25 g) **dark chocolate**, chopped
1 oz. (25 g) **candied orange peel**,
diced, plus more for decorating
7 oz. (200 g) **sponge cake**

FOR THE MARASCHINO SYRUP
2/3 cup (125 g) **sugar**

4 1/2 tbsp. (65 ml) **water**
3 tbsp. (40 ml) **maraschino cherry liqueur**

FOR THE ICING
1 cup (100 g) **confectioners' sugar**, sifted
1 tbsp. (15 ml) **water**
2-3 drops **lemon juice**
3 1/2 oz. (100 g) **marzipan**
Green food coloring, as needed

Strain the ricotta in a sieve, put it in a bowl and cream with the sugar. Add the candied orange peel and the chocolate and stir. Line the inside of a 9-inch cake pan or dessert mold with plastic wrap or waxed paper, leaving a 3-inch overhang. Cut the sponge cake into 2 layers and place 1 layer on the bottom of the dessert mold. Boil the water with the sugar in a saucepan to make the maraschino syrup. When the syrup has cooled to lukewarm, combine with the cherry liqueur. Moisten both layers of the sponge cake with this syrup. Spoon the ricotta cream over the sponge cake in the pan, spreading evenly. Place the other layer of moistened sponge cake on top. Refrigerate covered cake for several hours. For the icing, beat together the confectioners' sugar, water and lemon juice until well combined. Using the overhang of plastic wrap or waxed paper, remove the cake from the mold. Spread icing over top and sides. Add a few drops of green food coloring to the marzipan, if desired. Roll out marzipan with a rolling pin to a thickness of about 1/16 inch (1 mm). Wrap the sides of the cassata with the marzipan, and trim edges. Decorate with candied orange peel, if desired.

CHIACCHIERE
(ANGEL WINGS)

Preparation time: 30 minutes   Resting time: 30 minutes
Cooking time: 3 minutes   Difficulty: easy

4 SERVINGS

2 cups (250 g) **flour**
2 1/2 tbsp. (20 g) **confectioners' sugar**,
plus more for dusting
1 large **egg**
1 1/2 tbsp. (25 g) **unsalted butter**,
melted and cooled
3 1/2 tbsp. (50 g) **milk**

1 tbsp. (15 ml) **grappa**
Salt
1/3 tsp. (1 1/2 g) **baking powder**
Zest of 1/2 **lemon**, *grated*
1 tsp. (5 ml) **vanilla extract**
Vegetable oil *for frying*

Sift the flour and baking powder together into a bowl.
In a large bowl, whisk the egg, butter, sugar, grappa, milk, vanilla and zest. Add the flour mixture to the egg mixture gradually, kneading until dough is smooth. Form dough into a ball, cover with lightly oiled plastic wrap and let it rest for at least 30 minutes.
On a clean work surface (or using a pasta machine), roll the dough out into thin sheets, about 1/8 inch (3 mm) thick.
Cut the pastry into rectangles or diamond shapes with a pastry cutter. To obtain the characteristic wing shape, make three incisions lengthwise in each pastry rectangle or diamond. Fold the upper corner of the rectangle (or the upper corner of the diamond) and insert it into the center incision.
Heat at least 1 inch of vegetable oil in a large pot until hot and shimmering. Fry the dough for about 3 minutes and drain it on paper towels.
Dust with powdered sugar before serving.

CRÈME BRÛLÉE

Preparation time: 15 minutes   Cooking time: 60-75 minutes
Resting time: 2 hours   Difficulty: medium

4 SERVINGS

5 *egg yolks*
5/8 cup (125 g) sugar
2 cups (500 ml) heavy cream
1 *vanilla bean*
3 1/2 tbsp. (40 g) light brown sugar

Heat the oven to 200°F (100°C).
Slice the vanilla bean open lengthwise, using the tip of a sharp knife, and add to
the cream in a medium saucepan. Bring to a boil over low heat.
Remove vanilla bean. Separately, beat the egg yolks with the sugar in a bowl until
foamy and pale yellow. Slowly stream the boiling cream into the egg yolk mixture,
stirring well but trying to avoid forming froth.
Pour the cream into small dessert molds or ramekins. Prepare a hot water bath:
Place ramekins in a deep baking pan. Fill pan with enough hot water to reach
halfway up ramekins. Bake in the oven until the cream has set, from 20 to 25
minutes. Transfer ramekins to a wire cooling rack, cool completely, then
refrigerate for at least 2 hours.
Sprinkle brown sugar on top of each crème and caramelize with a culinary torch,
or place 4 inches under hot oven broiler until they are light brown.

CRÈME CARAMEL

Preparation time: 15 minutes   Cooking time: 35-40 minutes
Resting time: 2 hours   Difficulty: easy

4 SERVINGS

2 large **eggs***, beaten*
3/8 cup (85 g) **sugar**
1 1/3 cups (330 ml) **milk**
Zest of 1/2 **lemon**
1/4 cup (50 g) **sugar for the caramel**

Heat the oven to 300°F (150°C).
In a saucepan over medium-high heat, combine sugar and a tablespoon of water and bring to a boil. Reduce heat to medium-high and cook until mixture is light brown and caramelized. Divide caramel evenly between 4 ramekins or small dessert molds, swirling to coat ramekins. Let cool.
In a saucepan, combine the milk and lemon zest and bring to a boil. Remove and discard zest.
In a bowl, add a quarter of the milk to the eggs and stir well. Then add the remaining milk. (This will help you avoid cooking the eggs.).
Pour the mixture into the ramekins or molds. Prepare a hot water bath: Place ramekins in a deep baking pan. Fill pan with enough hot water to reach halfway up ramekins. Bake for 35 to 40 minutes.
Transfer ramekins to a wire cooling rack, cool completely, then refrigerate for at least 2 hours.
Before serving, invert each mold onto a dessert plate to serve crème with caramel on top.

WHITE CHOCOLATE
AND RASPBERRY TART

Preparation time: 1 hour 5 minutes Resting time: 2 hours
Cooking time: 18-20 minutes Difficulty: medium

4 SERVINGS

FOR THE CHOCOLATE SHORTBREAD CRUST
1 1/4 cups (165 g) **all-purpose flour**
1 1/2 sticks (95 g) **unsalted butter,**
softened
3/8 cup (85 g) **sugar**
2 large **egg yolks**
1/4 tsp. (1 g) **baking powder**
2 tbsp. plus 1 tsp. (9 g) **unsweetened**
cocoa powder
1/2 tsp. (3 ml) **vanilla extract**
Salt

FOR THE FILLING
3/8 cup (100 ml) **heavy cream**
2 tsp. (10 ml) **light corn syrup**
7 oz. (200 g) **white chocolate**
3 oz. (80 g) **raspberry jam**

FOR THE TOPPING
9 oz. (250 g) **fresh raspberries**
Confectioners' sugar

Prepare the crust. With an electric mixer, cream the butter and sugar, then stir in a pinch of salt, the egg yolks and the vanilla extract. Sift the flour with the baking powder and cocoa; add to the butter mixture, then knead briefly until you have a smooth dough. Form dough into a disk. Wrap in lightly oiled plastic wrap and refrigerate for 1 hour. Heat the oven to 360°F (180°C). Butter and flour a tart pan with a removable bottom. On a clean, lightly floured work surface, roll out the dough to 1/8 inch (3 mm) thick. Line tart pan with the dough. Spread with raspberry jam and bake for 18 to 20 minutes. Transfer tart pan to a wire rack to cool. Remove tart shell from the pan. Chop the white chocolate and put it in a heatproof bowl. Bring the cream and the corn syrup to a boil in a saucepan and pour it over the chocolate. Mix until you have a smooth, velvety cream. Let cool and pour into the tart shell (it should reach the brim). Top with raspberries and refrigerate for at least 1 hour. Sprinkle with confectioners' sugar before serving.

CHOCOLATE RICOTTA TART

Preparation time: 1 hour 5 minutes   Resting time: 2 hours
Cooking time: 25-30 minutes   Difficulty: medium

4 SERVINGS

FOR THE CRUST
1 1/4 cups (165 g) **all-purpose flour**
1/2 cup (100 g) **unsalted butter**
3/8 cup (85 g) **sugar**
1 large **egg**
1/4 tsp. (1 g) **baking powder** (optional)
1/2 tsp. (3 ml) **vanilla extract**
Salt

FOR THE FILLING
5 oz. (150 g) **ricotta**

2 tbsp. (30 g) **unsalted butter**, melted
and cooled
3 tbsp. (35 g) **sugar**
4 tsp. (10 g) **all-purpose flour**, sifted
Salt
1/2 tsp. (3 ml) **vanilla extract**

FOR THE GANACHE
3/8 cup (100 ml) **heavy cream**
2 tsp. (10 ml) **light corn syrup**
3 1/2 oz. (100 g) **dark chocolate**

Prepare the crust. With an electric mixer, cream the butter and sugar, then stir in a pinch of salt, the egg and the vanilla extract. Sift the flour with the baking powder; add to the butter mixture, then knead briefly until you have a smooth dough. Form dough into a disk. Wrap dough in lightly oiled plastic wrap and refrigerate for 1 hour. Heat the oven to 360°F (180°C).

On a clean, floured work surface, roll out disk of dough to 1/8 inch (3 mm) thick. Butter and flour a tart pan with a removable bottom. Line pan with the dough. For the filling, pass the ricotta through a sieve, then knead in a bowl with sugar, vanilla extract and a pinch of salt. Add the flour, then the butter. Mix well, then add to tart pan and bake for 25 to 30 minutes. Transfer tart pan to wire rack to cool. Remove tart from pan. For the ganache, chop the chocolate and place in a bowl. Bring the cream and the corn syrup to a boil in a saucepan and pour mixture over the chocolate. Mix until you have a smooth, velvety cream. Let cool and pour into the tart shell (it should reach the brim). Refrigerate for at least 1 hour.

RICH SHORTBREAD COOKIES

Preparation time: 15 minutes   Resting time: 1 hour
Cooking time: 18 minutes   Difficulty: easy

MAKES 1 LB. 7 OZ. (650 G) SHORTBREAD

1 1/4 cups (250 g) **unsalted butter,** *softened*
1 1/4 cups (125 g) **confectioners' sugar**
5 large hard-cooked **egg yolks**
2 1/2 cups (300 g) **all-purpose flour**
3/4 cup (100 g) **cornstarch**
1 **vanilla bean**
Salt

For hard-cooked egg yolks, cover eggs with water in a saucepan and bring to a boil over high heat. Reduce heat to low and simmer for 8 to 10 minutes. Drain eggs and immediately plunge them in cold water to stop the cooking process and make them easier to peel. Peel the eggs, then separate the yolks from the whites (which are not used in this recipe).

Slice the vanilla bean lengthwise and scrape out the seeds from one half bean (reserve other half bean for another use). Whisk the flour, the vanilla seeds and a pinch of salt in a bowl. Cream the butter and confectioners' sugar.

Run the egg yolks through a sieve. Mix them into the butter mixture until completely incorporated. Add the flour mixture. Knead the mixture until it is a smooth dough. Wrap the dough in lightly oiled plastic wrap and refrigerate for at least 1 hour. Heat the oven to 350°F (170°C).

On a lightly floured work surface, roll out the dough with a rolling pin to 1/6 inch (4 mm) thick. With a cookie cutter, cut into desired shapes.

Line a baking sheet with parchment paper. Arrange the shortbread cookies on the baking sheet and bake for about 18 minutes or until golden brown.

MOSCATO JELLY
WITH MIXED BERRIES

Preparation time: 10 minutes   Cooling time: 2 hours   Difficulty: easy

4 SERVINGS

1 1/2 cups plus 1 tbsp. (375 ml) **Moscato wine**
4 (10 g) **gelatin sheets** *or 1* **envelope granulated gelatin** *(1/4 oz.)*
4 1/2 oz. (125 g) **mixed berries**, *or about 1 cup*
4 **fresh mint leaves**

If you are using gelatin sheets, soak them in cold water. When softened, remove from the water and squeeze out excess liquid. In a small pot let gelatin dissolve in a few tablespoons of warmed Moscato, then stir in the remaining wine. Place a portion of mixed berries in individual serving bowls or parfait glasses and pour the liquid over them.

Refrigerate for at least 2 hours. Garnish with fresh mint leaves and serve.

CHOCOLATE ICE CREAM

Preparation time: 20 minutes   *Resting time: 6 hours*   *Difficulty: medium*

4 SERVINGS

2 cups (500 ml) **milk**
3/4 cup (150 g) **sugar**
5/8 cup (50 g) **unsweetened cocoa powder**
3 large **egg yolks**
1/3 oz. (10 g) **dark chocolate**, chopped

In a saucepan, heat the milk to 115°F (45°C), using an instant-read thermometer.
In a bowl, whisk together the sugar and cocoa, then pour the dry mixture into the milk; whisk again to combine.
Heat mixture to 150°F (65°C), whisk in the egg yolks and cook, stirring, for 10 seconds. Add the dark chocolate, stirring until melted.
Cool rapidly to 40°F (4°C) by putting the mixture in a container and immersing it in a bowl of ice water.
Refrigerate the ice cream base for 6 hours, then process in an ice cream maker according to manufacturer's instructions.
Transfer ice cream to an airtight container and place in freezer until firm.

VANILLA ICE CREAM

Preparation time: 20 minutes   Resting time: 6 hours   Difficulty: easy

4 SERVINGS

2 cups (500 ml) **milk**
3/4 cup (150 g) **sugar**
2 tbsp. (15 g) **powdered skim milk**
5 large **egg yolks (90 g)**
3 1/2 tbsp. (50 ml) **heavy cream**
1/2 **vanilla bean**

Scrape seeds from the vanilla bean. In a saucepan, combine vanilla bean with the milk and heat to 115°F (45°C), using an instant-read thermometer. In a bowl, whisk together the sugar and powdered milk, then gradually sprinkle the mixture into the milk, whisking to combine. Heat mixture to 150°F (65°C), whisk together the egg yolks and cream, then whisk into the milk and cook, stirring, for 10 seconds. Cool rapidly to 40°F (4°C) by putting the mixture in a container and immersing it in a bowl of ice water.

Refrigerate for 6 hours, remove the vanilla bean, then process in an ice cream maker, according to manufacturer's instructions, until thick. Transfer to an airtight container and place in freezer until firm.

COFFEE GRANITA

Preparation time: 2 hours   Difficulty: easy

4 SERVINGS

2/3 cup (150 ml) **espresso**
1 cup (255 ml) **water**
2/3 cup (100 g) **sugar**

Dissolve the sugar in the hot coffee. Add the water and let the liquid cool. Pour mixture into a heatproof bowl and put it in the freezer.
From time to time, whisk the contents of the bowl to break up any frozen clumps. The granita is ready when the ice reaches a uniform consistency and granularity. Remove from the freezer and serve in dessert bowls.

ORANGE GRANITA

Preparation time: 4 hours   Difficulty: easy

4 SERVINGS

1 cup (250 ml) **water**
1/4 cup plus 2 tbsp. (75 g) **sugar**
3 1/2 tbsp. (50 ml) **lemon juice**
2 **oranges**

Rinse and zest the oranges. Grate the zest, being careful not to include any of the bitter white pith. Juice the oranges, filtering the juice with a fine-mesh strainer.

Make a syrup by boiling the water and sugar for 4 to 5 minutes. Let it cool and combine it with the citrus juices and orange zest.

Freeze the liquid for about 1 hour, until ice crystals start to form. Whisk it well and return it to the freezer. Repeat this process at least 4 or 5 times. The granita is ready when the ice reaches a uniform consistency and granularity.

Garnish with orange zest, if desired, and serve in dessert bowls.

MERINGUES

Preparation time: 20 minutes   Cooking time: 1 1/2 to 2 hours
Difficulty: easy

4 SERVINGS

3 large **egg whites**, *at room temperature*
1 cup (200 g) **sugar**

Heat the oven to 200°F (100°C).
In a clean bowl, beat the egg whites and 1/4 cup of the sugar until egg whites
form stiff, glossy peaks. Gently fold in the remaining 3/4 cup of sugar.
Line a baking sheet with parchment paper.
Put the meringue mixture in a pastry bag with a 1/2-inch tip. Pipe the meringue
into 1 1/2-inch-diameter cookies onto prepared baking sheet lined.
Bake for 1 1/2 to 2 hours or until the meringues are completely dry.
Store the meringues in an airtight container.

MILK CHOCOLATE MOUSSE

Preparation time: 1 hour 20 minutes   Cooling time: 3 hours   Difficulty: medium

6 SERVINGS

FOR THE MOUSSE
1 cup (250 ml) **milk**
2 large **egg yolks**
9 oz. (250 g) **milk chocolate**, chopped
7 oz. (200 g) **heavy cream**
4 (10 g) **gelatin sheets**, or 1 **envelope granulated gelatin** (1/4 oz.)

FOR CHOCOLATE CRUST
1/2 cup (100 g) **sugar**
3 large **eggs**, separated, plus one large **egg yolk**

2/3 cup (80 g) **all-purpose flour**
2 1/2 tbsp. (20 g) **cornstarch**
3 tbsp. (15 g) **unsweetened cocoa powder**

FOR THE SYRUP
2 tbsp. (30 ml) **water**
3/8 cup (80 g) **sugar**
2 1/2 tbsp. (35 ml) **rum** (or other liqueur of your choice)

Heat oven to 450°F (230°C). For the crust, sift together flour, cornstarch, and cocoa. Beat the egg whites with the sugar in a clean bowl until soft peaks form. In a separate bowl, whisk egg yolks until fluffy. Fold whites into the yolks, followed by the flour mixture. Spread a layer of dough about 3/8 inch (1 cm) thick on a 12-inch (30 1/2 cm) baking sheet lined with parchment. Bake 5 to 7 minutes. For mousse, put the chocolate in a bowl. If you are using gelatin sheets, soak them in cold water until softened, then squeeze out excess liquid. In a saucepan over low heat, combine egg yolks and milk and heat to 185°F (85°C), stirring constantly. Remove from heat and add gelatin, stirring to dissolve. Pour this mixture into the chocolate and stir until smooth. Let cool to 86°F (30°C). For the syrup, boil the water and sugar in a pan, cool, then stir in the rum. Whip the cream until soft peaks form, then fold into chocolate-mousse mixture. Line a cake ring with baked dough, trim excess, and pour syrup on crust to soak it. Fill crust with mousse. Smooth surface and refrigerate for 3 hours. Remove from pan.

WHITE CHOCOLATE MOUSSE
WITH PEACH JELLY

Preparation time: 1 1/2 hours   Cooling time: 2 hours   Difficulty: medium

4 SERVINGS

FOR THE MOUSSE
*1 cup (125 ml) **heavy cream***
*9 oz. (250 g) **white chocolate**, chopped*

FOR THE PEACH JELLY
*9 oz. (250 g) **yellow peaches**, peeled,*
pitted, and cut into small pieces
*1/3 cup (75 g) **sugar***
*3 (8 g) **gelatin sheets** or 3/4 envelope*
granulated gelatin

For the peach jelly, soften the gelatin sheets in cold water, then squeeze out excess liquid. (If you are using granulated gelatin, dissolve it directly in the hot peach purée.)

Purée the peaches in a blender. In a saucepan, bring the sugar and one-third of peach purée to a boil.

Dissolve gelatin in peach mixture. Add remaining peach purée and stir to combine. Pour jelly into individual serving cups or bowls, and let cool.

For the mousse, put chopped chocolate in a bowl. Boil 1/2 cup cream in a saucepan and pour over the chocolate, stirring until it is smooth and creamy. Cool to 85°F (30°C).

In the meantime, whip the cream in a clean bowl until it forms soft peaks. Whip the remaining 1/2 cup of cream until soft peaks form. Gently fold the whipped cream into the chocolate mixture.

Top the servings of peach jelly with the mousse. Refrigerate for at least 2 hours. Garnish with shavings of white chocolate, if desired.

PANNA COTTA

Preparation time: 20 minutes   Resting time: 3 hours   Difficulty: easy

4 SERVINGS

1/2 cup (125 ml) **milk**
1/2 cup (125 ml) **heavy cream**
1/4 cup (50 g) **sugar**
4 (10 g) **gelatin sheets** *or 1 envelope* **granulated gelatin** *(1/4 oz.)*

Bring the milk, cream and sugar to a boil in a saucepan.
If you are using gelatin sheets, soften them in cold water, then squeeze out excess liquid. Add gelatin to milk mixture, stirring well to prevent froth from forming. Pour mixture into individual dessert molds. Refrigerate for at least 3 hours.
Remove from the molds. Panna cotta can be served with a chocolate or caramel sauce, or with a fruit sauce made with berries, kiwis, or pears. Hazelnuts or pistachios are other common toppings.

NEAPOLITAN EASTER PIE

Preparation time: 50 minutes   Cooking time: 40 minutes
Resting time: 1 hour   Difficulty: high

4 SERVINGS

FOR THE CRUST
1 1/2 cups (200 g) **all-purpose flour**
7 tbsp. (100 g) **unsalted butter**, softened
1/2 cup (100 g) **sugar**
1/2 tsp. (2 g) **baking powder**
1 large **egg**
Zest of 1 **lemon**, grated
1 pinch **salt**

FOR THE CONFECTIONERS' CREAM
1 large **egg yolk**
1/2 cup (55 g) **sugar**
2 tbsp. plus 1 tsp. (18 g) **all-purpose flour**
7/8 cups (200 ml) **milk**

FOR THE FILLING
8 3/4 oz. (250 g) **ricotta**
3/4 cup (75 g) **confectioners' sugar**
1 cup (225 g) **confectioners' cream**
1 large **egg yolk**
5 oz. (150 g) **"grano cotto per
pastiera"** (special cooked wheat for
pastiera) or cooked pearled barley.
1 3/4 oz. (50 g) **candied citron**, diced
Orange blossom water (or finely grated
orange zest), as needed

In a food processor, pulse butter and sugar. Add the egg, lemon zest and salt and pulse. Sift flour with baking powder and pulse with butter mixture until crumbs form. Knead until dough is smooth. Form into 2 balls, 1 larger, wrap in plastic, and refrigerate for 1 hour. On a floured surface, roll out larger ball to 1/10 inch (3 mm) thick. Line a springform pan with dough; trim edges. For confectioners' cream, beat egg yolk with sugar, add flour and stir. Bring milk to a boil and add egg mixture. Return to a boil, then cool. Pass ricotta through a sieve and add powdered sugar, confectioners' cream, egg yolk, cooked wheat, citron and orange blossom water. Stir. Pour filling into crust. Heat oven to 360°F (180°C). Roll out smaller dough. Cut into 10 1/2-inch-wide strips. Place 5 strips across top and strips at right angles to first strips. Trim; pinch to seal. Bake for about 1 1/2 hours. Let pie cool completely before removing it from pan.

PEACHES STUFFED
WITH AMARETTI COOKIES

Preparation time: 20 minutes   Cooking time: 30 minutes   Difficulty: easy

4 SERVINGS

4 **peaches**
5 **amaretti cookies**, *crushed*
3 tbsp. plus 2 tsp. (20 g) **unsweetened cocoa powder**
2 large **eggs**, *separated*
1/4 cup plus 1 1/2 tbsp. (70 g) **sugar**

Heat the oven to 325°F (160°C).
Rinse, halve and pit peaches. Use a spoon to scoop out some flesh from each half, leaving enough of the peach intact to form a "cup." Chop extracted peach flesh and mix it with the 2 egg yolks, amaretti crumbs, and cocoa.
Beat the egg whites with the sugar until stiff peaks form.
Fold whites into the peach-amaretti mixture.
Fill the peach halves with the mixture, transfer to a baking pan lined with parchment paper, and bake for about 30 minutes.
Stuffed peaches can be served warm or at room temperature.

CHOCOLATE PROFITEROLES

Preparation time: 1 1/2 hours   Difficulty: high

4 SERVINGS

FOR THE PASTRY CREAM
1 large **egg yolk**
3 1/2 tbsp. (40 g) **sugar**
4 tsp. (10 g) **all-purpose flour**, sifted
1/2 cup (125 ml) **milk**
1/4 **vanilla bean**, seeds scraped

FOR THE PASTRY PUFFS
6 3/4 (100 ml) **water**
3 1/2 tbsp. (50 g) **unsalted butter**, cut
into small pieces

1/2 cup (60 g) **all-purpose flour**, sifted
2 large **eggs**
Salt

FOR THE CHOCOLATE SAUCE
3/8 cup (100 ml) **whipped cream**
3 1/2 oz. (100 g) **dark chocolate**,
chopped

Heat oven to 400°F (200°C). For pastry puffs, bring the water, butter, and a pinch of salt to a boil in a saucepan. Add flour and stir until mixture pulls away from side of pan and forms a ball, about 30 seconds. Transfer mixture to a bowl and cool slightly. Add eggs, 1 at a time, beating well after each addition. Butter and flour a baking sheet. Transfer mixture to a pastry bag with a large plain tip and pipe mounds about 1 1/4 inches wide and 1 inch high. Bake until puffed and golden brown, about 20 minutes. Prick each pastry with a skewer, then return to oven to dry, leaving oven door slightly ajar, 3 minutes. Transfer sheet to a rack to cool. For the pastry cream, heat the milk in a saucepan with the vanilla bean. Whisk egg yolks and sugar together in a bowl, then add flour and stir. Remove vanilla bean. Pour a little hot milk on the egg mixture, mix, then slowly add the remainder and combine. Return to saucepan and bring to a boil. Remove from heat and let cool. Combine the whipped cream with 1/2 cup (120 ml) pastry cream. When cool, tranfer pastry cream to a piping bag, with a small plain tip and fill puffs. Refrigerate until ready to serve. For chocolate sauce, put the chocolate in a bowl. Bring the cream to a boil in a saucepan and pour it over the chocolate. Stir to obtain a smooth cream. Dizzle cream puffs with sauce.

CHOCOLATE DESSERT "SALAMI"

Preparation time: 3 hours   Difficulty: easy

MAKES ONE SALAMI

2 oz. (50 g) **plain biscotti**, *coarsely crushed*
5 tsp. (25 g) **unsalted butter**, *softened*
4 oz. (120 g) **dark chocolate with hazelnuts**, *chopped*
1 tbsp. (10 g) **roasted hazelnuts**
1 tbsp. (10 g) **pistachios**
1 tbsp. (10 g) **pine nuts**
1 tbsp. (10 g) **sweet almonds**
Confectioners' sugar

In a bowl, combine the biscotti, toasted hazelnuts, pistachios, pine nuts, and sweet almonds.

Melt the dark chocolate with hazelnuts with the butter in a bowl set over a pan of simmering water. Let it cool slightly, then pour over biscotti-and-nut mixture. Let the mixture harden just enough so that you can still mix and manipulate it. On a work surface dusted with confectioners' sugar, form the chocolate mixture into a sausage shape.

Sprinkle more confectioners' sugar over the chocolate salami. Wrap it in waxed paper, tying it with kitchen string to resemble a meat salami, if desired.

CHOCOLATE-COVERED
ORANGE PEELS

Preparation time: 12 hours   Difficulty: easy

4 SERVINGS

*4 1/2 oz. (130 g) **candied orange peel***
*2 1/2 oz. (70 g) **dark chocolate***

Quarter the candied orange peels and place on a wire rack to dry at room temperature overnight.

When orange peels are dry, cut them into strips about 1/4 inch (6 mm) wide.

Temper the dark chocolate: Melt the chocolate in a heatproof bowl set over a pan of simmering water until chocolate reaches 110°–120°F (45°–50°C) on a candy thermometer. (Or microwave chocolate in 15-second increments, stirring in between, until chocolate reaches desired temperature.)

Pour one third to one half of chocolate onto a marble surface or metal baking sheet set over an ice pack. Let cool until it reaches 79°–81°F (26°–27°C), then return cooled chocolate to the remaining hot chocolate. When this mixture reaches 86°–88°F (30°–31°C), it is ready to be used.

Use a fork to dip the candied orange peels into the tempered chocolate. Drain the excess chocolate and place the coated peels on a sheet of parchment paper or waxed paper to set at room temperature.

VANILLA SEMIFREDDO

Preparation time: 1 hour   Freezing time: 3 hours   Difficulty: medium

4 SERVINGS

2 cups (500 ml) **heavy cream**, *chilled*

1 **vanilla bean**, *split lengthwise*

FOR THE SEMIFREDDO BASE
7 large **egg yolks**, *at room temperature*
2/3 cup (130 g) **sugar**
2 1/2 tbsp. (35 ml) **water**
6 **gelatin sheets**, *or 1 1/2 envelopes*
granulated gelatin *(3/8 oz.)*

FOR THE ITALIAN-STYLE MERINGUE
2 large **egg whites**, *at room*
temperature
1/2 cup (100 g) **sugar**
4 tsp. (20 ml) **water**

For the meringue, heat the water and 1/3 cup sugar in a pan over medium heat.
Meanwhile, beat the egg whites with the remaining sugar until stiff peaks form.
When the sugar mixture on the stove has reached 250°F (121°C) on a candy
thermometer, combine it with the egg whites and continue beating until the
mixture is lukewarm. Set aside. If you are using gelatin sheets, soak them in cold
water until softened, then squeeze out excess liquid.
For the semifreddo base, cook the sugar with the water until it reaches 250°F
(121°C) on a candy thermometer, then beat in the egg yolks. Add the gelatin to
the mixture, scrape the seeds of the vanilla bean into it and continue beating
until the mixture is cool. Combine the meringue and semifreddo base, and fold
in the heavy cream.
Pour into individual dessert molds and place in the freezer for 3 hours.
Unmold and serve.

LEMON SORBET

Preparation time: 30 minutes   Freezing time: 6 hours   Difficulty: easy

FOR APPROXIMATELY 2 PINTS (1 L) OF ICE CREAM

2 cups (440 ml) **water**
3/4 cup (190 ml) **lemon juice**
1 cup **sugar**
1 tbsp. (5 g) **lemon zest**

Bring the water to a boil in a pan. Pour sugar in a steady stream into the boiling water, whisking well until the mixture reaches 150°F (65°C) on a candy thermometer. Remove from heat and let cool. When simple syrup is cool, add the lemon juice and zest; stir to combine. Cool rapidly to 40°F (4°C) by putting the mixture in a container and immersing it in a bowl of ice water. Refrigerate for 6 hours, then process in an ice cream maker until thick, according to manufacturer's instructions. Transfer to an airtight container and freeze until ready to serve.

RICOTTA MOUSSE

Preparation time: 1 hour   Chilling time: 11 hours   Difficulty: medium

4 SERVINGS

9 oz. (250 g) **ricotta**
2/3 cup (160 ml) **heavy cream**
3 1/2 oz. (100 g) **unsalted almonds**, *or about 1 cup finely ground*
1/4 cup plus 2 tbsp. (75 g) **sugar**
2 large **egg yolks**
2 **gelatin sheets** *(5 g), or 1/2* **envelope of granulated gelatin** *(1/8 oz.)*
1 1/4 cups (300 ml) **water**

Mix the ground almonds with the water. Refrigerate the mixture for about 8 hours to make almond milk. Strain the almond milk through cheesecloth. Beat the egg yolks with the sugar and stir in 1/2 cup (125 ml) of almond milk. Transfer to a pan over medium heat and let the mixture thicken, stirring occasionally. If you are using gelatin sheets, soak them in water until softened; squeeze out excess water. Dissolve gelatin in the hot almond-milk mixture. Let mixture cool and stir in the ricotta. In a bowl, whip the cream and fold it into the ricotta mixture.
Pour into individual dessert molds and freeze for about 3 hours. Unmold and serve chilled.

APPLE STRUDEL

Preparation time: 1 hour   Cooking time: 20 minutes
Resting time: 30 minutes   Difficulty: medium

4 SERVINGS

FOR THE DOUGH
2 cups (250 g) **all-purpose flour**
2/3 cup (150 ml) **water**
1 tbsp. plus 1 tsp. (20 ml) **extra-virgin olive oil**
Salt

FOR THE FILLING
1 3/4 lbs. (800 g) **tart apples**, such as Granny Smith
3 1/2 oz. (100 g) **raisins**, or about 2/3 cup packed

3 1/2 oz. (100 g) **pine nuts**, or about 2/3 cup
1/2 stick (60 g) **unsalted butter**
2-3 1/2 oz. (60-100 g) **breadcrumbs**
Cinnamon

FOR TOPPING
1 large **egg**, lightly beaten
Confectioners' sugar, as needed
Whipped cream, if desired

On a clean work surface, combine flour, water, oil and a pinch of salt; knead until dough is smooth. Form it into a ball, cover with lightly oiled plastic wrap and let rest for at least 30 minutes. Meanwhile, prepare filling. Peel and slice apples. Soak raisins in lukewarm water for 15 minutes; drain and squeeze out excess water. In a skillet over medium heat, melt butter and sauté apple slices, raisins, pine nuts and a pinch of cinnamon. Add just enough breadcrumbs to hold mixture together. Heat the oven to 350°F (175°C). On a floured work surface, roll dough into a thin rectangle 12 inches (30 1/2 cm) long by 8 (18 cm) inches wide, then stretch it with your hands. Spoon filling along long side, leaving a 2-inch (5 cm) border. Roll dough over filling into a log, pressing down along the edges with your fingers to seal and curling up the ends. Brush strudel with the egg, place it in a baking pan lined with parchment and bake until golden brown (about 20 minutes), dusting with confectioners' sugar a few minutes before removing from oven. Serve with whipped cream, if desired.

ASSORTED TRUFFLES

Preparation time: 45 minutes   Cooling time: 4 hours   Difficulty: easy

4 SERVINGS

FOR DARK CHOCOLATE TRUFFLES
2 1/4 oz. (65 g) **dark chocolate**, chopped
3/8 cup (50 g) **toasted hazelnuts**, chopped
1 cup (100 g) **confectioners' sugar**
1/8 cup (12 g) **unsweetened cocoa powder**
4 tsp. (20 ml) **light extra-virgin olive oil**
Sweetened or unsweetened cocoa
powder, for dusting

FOR WHITE CHOCOLATE TRUFFLES
2 oz. (60 g) **white chocolate**, chopped
4 1/2 tbsp. (60 g) **hazelnut paste**

3 tbsp. (25 g) **toasted hazelnuts**, chopped
5/8 cup (65 g) **confectioners' sugar**, plus
more for dusting
2 tsp. (2 g) **unsweetened cocoa powder**

FOR PISTACHIO TRUFFLES
7 oz. (200 g) **white chocolate**, chopped
3 1/2 tbsp. (30 g) **pistachios**, chopped,
plus 3/8 cup (50 g) **chopped** for topping
4 tsp. (25 g) **pistachio paste**
Confectioners' sugar, for work surface

For dark chocolate truffles, melt chocolate in a heatproof bowl set over a pan of simmering water. Mix in remaining ingredients, adding oil as needed, until smooth. Let mixture cool for 4 hours at room temperature. On a work surface dusted with cocoa, roll cooled chocolate into lengths, cut into 1-inch pieces. Form the pieces into balls and roll them in cocoa. For white truffles, melt chocolate as directed above, then mix in all ingredients but confectioners' sugar. Cool as above. On a work surface dusted with confectioners' sugar, roll cooled chocolate into lengths, cut into 1-inch pieces and form into balls. Dust with confectioners' sugar. For pistachio truffles, melt 3 1/2 ounces of chocolate as above, then stir in pistachio paste and 3 1/2 tbsp. chopped pistachios. Cool as above. On a work surface dusted with confectioners' sugar, roll cooled chocolate into lengths, cut into 1-inch pieces and form into balls. Melt remaining chocolate, cool and dip truffles to coat. Roll truffles in 3/8 cup chopped pistachios.

TIRAMISÙ

Preparation time: 30 minutes   Resting time: 2 hours   Difficulty: medium

4 SERVINGS

*4 large **egg yolks***
*2 large **egg whites***
*1/2 cup plus 2 tbsp. (125 g) **sugar***
*1 cup (250 g) **mascarpone***
*1 tbsp. plus 2 tsp. (25 ml) **brandy** (optional)*
*1 cup (200 ml) **sweetened coffee***
*8 **ladyfingers** (savoiardi)*
***Unsweetened cocoa powder**, as needed*

Beat the egg yolks with three-quarters of the sugar in a heatproof bowl until thick and pale, then set over a pan of simmering water until warmed through. Remove from heat.
In another bowl, beat the egg whites with the remaining sugar until stiff peaks form.
Stir the mascarpone into the egg yolk mixture, then gently fold in egg white mixture, letting it remain light and frothy.
Dip the ladyfingers in the sweetened coffee (add brandy, if desired). Transfer 4 ladyfingers to an 8-inch glass baking dish or 4 small dessert bowls (2 ladyfingers per bowl). Pour in a layer of the cream mixture, alternating with another layer of ladyfingers and ending with cream.
Refrigerate tiramisù, covered, for about two hours.
Top with a generous dusting of cocoa powder.

CHOCOLATE ALMOND CAKE

Preparation time: 30 minutes   Cooking time: 45 minutes   Difficulty: easy

4 SERVINGS

5 tbsp. (70 g) **unsalted butter**, softened
5/8 cup (60 g) **confectioners' sugar**, *plus more for dusting*
1 large **egg**, *separated, plus* 1 large **egg yolk**
2 1/2 oz. (75 g) **dark chocolate**, *chopped*
1/3 cup (50 g) **blanched almonds**

Heat the oven to 325°F (160°C).
In a food processor, grind the almonds with a quarter of the sugar. Set aside.
Melt the chocolate in a heatproof bowl set over a pan of simmering water.
In a separate bowl, cream the butter and the remaining sugar until pale and fluffy. Add the egg yolks and continue beating.
Add the warm, melted chocolate to the egg-yolk mixture, then add the ground almonds and stir.
Beat the egg white and gently fold into the chocolate mixture.
Butter and flour an 8-inch cake pan (or line with parchment paper). Pour cake batter to fill three-quarters of pan. Bake for 40 to 45 minutes, or until a cake tester inserted in middle comes out clean.
Move the pan to a wire rack to cool. Remove cake from pan and dust with confectioners' sugar.

CRUMBLY CAKE
(SBRISOLONA)

Preparation time: 20 minutes   *Cooking time: 18 minutes*   *Difficulty: easy*

4 SERVINGS

3/4 cup plus 1 tbsp. (100 g) **all-purpose flour**
1/4 cup (25 g) **finely ground cornmeal**
6 tbsp. (75 g) **sugar**
2/3 stick (75 g) **unsalted butter**, softened
2 2/3 oz. (75 g) **ground almonds**
1 large **egg yolk**
1 pinch **baking powder**
12 **whole unpeeled almonds**
Grated **lemon zest** *to taste*

Heat the oven to 350°F (175°C).
Put the flour, butter, sugar, eggs, baking powder, lemon zest and cormeal in a
large bowl. Knead to obtain a crumbly dough.
Put the mixture in a greased 9-inch baking pan.
Scatter whole almonds on top of the crumble mixture.
Bake in the oven for 20 to 25 minutes, or until golden.

VIENNESE CAKE

Preparation time: 45 minutes   Cooking time: 40-45 minutes   Difficulty: high

4-6 SERVINGS

FOR THE CAKE
4 oz. (115 g) **blanched almonds**
2/3 cup (137 g) **sugar**
3/8 cup (45 g) **all-purpose flour**
1 1/2 tbsp. (12 g) **cornstarch**
1/4 cup (25 g) **cocoa powder**
Salt
1/2 tsp. (3 ml) **vanilla extract**
3 oz. (80 g) **dark chocolate**
5 tsp. (25 g) **unsalted butter**, softened
4 large **eggs**, separated, plus 1 large
egg yolk

FOR THE FILLING
4 oz. (120 g) **apricot jam**
4 tsp. (20 ml) **orange liqueur**, such as
Grand Marnier

FOR THE CHOCOLATE GANACHE
2/3 cup (170 ml) **cream**
6 oz. (170 g) **bittersweet chocolate**,
finely chopped

Heat oven to 360°F (180°C). In a food processor, finely grind almonds with 2 tablespoons (25 g) of sugar. Mix in a bowl with flour, cornstarch, cocoa, and a pinch of salt. Melt the chocolate and butter in a heatproof bowl set over a pan of simmering water. In a separate bowl, beat yolks with vanilla and 4 tablespoons (50 g) sugar. In another bowl, beat egg whites with 1/3 cup (62 g) sugar. Lighten the yolks with one-third of the whites, then add melted chocolate and butter. Combine with dry ingredients. Fold in remaining egg whites. Pour into a greased, floured loaf pan. Bake in the oven for 40 minutes, or until cake tester comes out clean. Transfer pan to rack to cool. When cool, remove cake from pan and cut horizontally into three layers. Place bottom layer on serving plate. Stir together apricot jam and orange liqueur. Spread mixture over top of first cake layer. Add second layer and spread filling over top. Add last cake layer. Put chopped chocolate in a bowl. Bring cream to a boil; pour over chocolate. Stir until you have a velvety frosting. Spread evenly over cake.

CHOCOLATE CUPCAKES
WITH ORANGE AND BANANA

Preparation time: 20 minutes   Cooking time: 20 minutes   Difficulty: easy

6 CUPCAKES

3 1/2 tbsp. (50 g) **unsalted butter**, softened
1/4 cup (50 g) **sugar**
1 oz. (30 g) **dark chocolate**, chopped
1 large **egg**
1/4 cup (60 ml) **milk**
3/4 cup (100 g) **all-purpose flour**, sifted
2 tbsp. (10 g) **unsweetened cocoa powder**
2 tsp. (5 g) **baking powder**
1 **orange**
1 **banana**
Salt

Heat oven to 340°F (170°C).

Melt chocolate in a heatproof bowl set over a pan of simmering water. Cool chocolate slightly.

Cream the butter and sugar together in a bowl, then whisk in the warm, melted chocolate. Whisk in the egg, milk, and a pinch of salt.

Stir in the flour with the cocoa and baking powder.

Peel the banana and cut it into slices.

Peel the orange and dice each segment.

Gently stir the fruit into the chocolate mixture.

Butter and flour 6 cups of a muffin pan. Pour batter evenly into pan. Bake for about 20 minutes, or until a cake tester inserted in the middle comes out clean. Remove from the oven and let cool.

"SOFT-HEARTED" CHOCOLATE CUPCAKES

Preparation time: 20 minutes   *Cooking time: 5-10 minutes*   *Difficulty: medium*

6 CUPCAKES

6 oz. (180 g) **dark chocolate**, *chopped*
3 tbsp. (40 g) **unsalted butter**
1/4 cup (50 g) **sugar**
3/8 cup (50 g) **all-purpose flour**
5 **egg whites**
2 **egg yolks**

In a heatproof bowl set over a pan of simmering water, melt the dark chocolate and butter.

Meanwhile, beat the egg whites in a bowl until frothy. Add the sugar and continue to beat until stiff peaks form.

Add the egg yolks to the egg whites and combine with the melted chocolate and butter.

Delicately fold in the sifted flour.

Butter and flour 6 cups of a muffin pan. Pour batter three-quarters of the way up each cup.

Cover and refrigerate until well chilled, or freeze.

When ready to serve, bake in the oven at 400°F (200°C) for 5 to 6 minutes (8 to 10 minutes, if the cupcakes were frozen).

Serve immediately, so that the centers (or hearts) of the cupcakes are still soft.

COLD ZABAGLIONE
WITH MOSCATO

Preparation time: 15 minutes   Cooking time: 10 minutes
Resting time: 2 hours   Difficulty: easy

4 SERVINGS

4 large **egg yolks**
2 tbsp. (25 g) **sugar**
3/4 cup (200 ml) **Moscato d'Asti** *or other Muscat wine*
7/8 cup (220 ml) **heavy cream**
2 **gelatin sheets**, *or 1/2* **envelope graulated gelatin** *(1/8 oz.)*

In a pan, preferably copper, beat the egg yolks lightly with the sugar and wine.
Place the pan over low heat (or in a heatproof bowl set over a pan of simmering water) and continue cooking until the mixture becomes frothy and has thickened into a custard.
Meanwhile, if you are using gelatin sheets, soak them in cold water until softened, then squeeze out any excess water.
Add the gelatin to the custard.
Remove from the heat and let cool.
Whip the cream and gently fold it into the cool zabaglione.
Pour into individual bowls and put in the refrigerator for at least 2 hours.
Garnish, as desired, with fresh berries, biscotti or chocolate shavings.

INGREDIENTS INDEX

PHOTO CREDITS

All photographs are by ACADEMIA BARILLA except the following:
pages 6, 95 ©123RF

· · · · · · · · · · · ·

The Taunton Press
Inspiration for hands-on living®

The Taunton Press, Inc.
63 South Main Street
PO Box 5506, Newtown, CT 06470-5506
e-mail: tp@taunton.com

Translations:
Catherine Howard - Mary Doyle - John Venerella - Free z'be, Paris
Salvatore Ciolfi - Rosetta Translations SARL - Rosetta Translations SARL

LIBRARY OF CONGRESS CATALOGING-IN-PUBLICATION DATA IN PROGRESS
ISBN: 978-1-62710-054-0

Printed in China
10 9 8 7 6 5 4 3 2 1